STUDY GUIDE

The Life of Samson

W. Robert Godfrey

LIGONIER MINISTRIES

Renew your Mind.

LIGONIER.ORG | 800-435-4343

Contents

Introduction

A man of incredible physical strength and debilitating moral weakness, Samson was nevertheless God's instrument to rescue Israel from the Philistines during the era of the judges. In light of these contrasts, we are faced with this key question: What, exactly, are we to make of Samson and his place in the Lord's purposes? In this series, Dr. W. Robert Godfrey considers the life of Samson, highlighting vital theological lessons and exploring what this judge tells us about Christian living.

This study guide is a companion to the video teaching series. Whether you are using the DVDs, streaming the videos on Ligonier.org, or going through the course in Ligonier Connect, this resource is designed to help you make the most of the learning experience. For each message in the series, there is a corresponding lesson in this guide. Here is what you will find in each lesson:

INTRODUCTION	The introduction is a brief paragraph that summarizes the content covered in the lecture and considered in the study guide lesson. **How to use:** Use the introduction to each lesson to get a sense of the big picture before watching the video. Refer to these statements as you work through the study guide to remind you of what have already covered and where you are headed.
LEARNING GOALS	The learning goals are the knowledge and skills the study guide lesson will endeavor to equip you with as you work through the lecture content. **How to use:** Familiarize yourself with the goals of each lesson before engaging its contents. Keeping the overall purpose in mind as you watch each video and reflect on or discuss the questions will help you get the most out of each lesson.
KEY IDEAS	The key ideas are the major points or takeaways from the lecture. **How to use:** Use these ideas to prepare yourself for each lesson and to review previous lessons. They describe specifically the knowledge each lecture is communicating.

REFLECTION & DISCUSSION QUESTIONS	The questions are the guided reflection and/or discussion component of the lesson that are intended to help you prepare for, process, and organize what you are learning. **How to use:** Reflect on individually or discuss in a group the questions in the order in which they appear in the lesson. The ▶ icon indicates where to play and pause the video for questions that address specific segments of the lecture.
PRAYER	The prayer section offers suggestions for how to close the lesson in prayer with respect to what was taught in the lecture. **How to use:** Consider using each lesson's prayer section as a guide to personal or group prayer. These sections follow the ACTS prayer model, which you can learn more about in R.C. Sproul's Crucial Questions booklet *Who Is the Holy Spirit?* This helpful guide is available as a free e-book at Ligonier.org.
REVIEW QUIZ	The review quiz is a set of six multiple-choice questions that appear at the end of each lesson. **How to use:** Use each quiz to check your comprehension and memory of the major points covered in each lecture. It will be most beneficial to your learning if you take a lesson's quiz either sometime between lessons or just before you begin the next lesson in the study guide.
ANSWER KEY	The answer key provides explanations for the reflection and discussion questions and answers to the multiple-choice questions in the review quiz. **How to use:** Use the answer key to check your own answers or when you do not know the answer. Note: Do not give in too quickly; struggling for a few moments to recall an answer reinforces it in your mind.

Study Schedules

The following table suggests four plans for working through *The Life of Samson* video teaching series and this companion study guide. Whether you are going through this series on your own or with a group, these schedules should help you plan your study path.

WEEK	Extended 12-Week Plan	Standard 10-Week Plan	Abbreviated 6-Week Plan	Intensive 4-Week Plan
	LESSON			
1	*	1	1	1–2
2	1	2	2 & 3	3–5
3	2	3	4 & 5	6–8
4	3	4	6 & 7	9–10
5	4	5	8 & 9	
6	5	6	10	
7	6	7		
8	7	8		
9	8	9		
10	9	10		
11	10			
12	*			

* For these weeks, rather than completing lessons, spend your time discussing and praying about your learning goals for the study (the first week) and the most valuable takeaways from the study (the last week).

1

The Riddle of Samson

INTRODUCTION

Samson is a puzzling character. What are we to make of him? Is he an example of faith or disobedience—or both? The English poet John Milton called Samson a "mirror of our fickle state." In this lesson, we will consider the reasons why the story of Samson deserves close examination and his place in the context of the book of Judges.

LEARNING GOALS

When you have finished this lesson, you should be able to:

- Identify the goals for this study of Samson
- Summarize the purpose of the book of Judges

KEY IDEAS

- Proper Bible study requires us to consider both the big picture of Scripture and the specific context of what we are studying.
- The book of Judges is a record of Israel's spiritual decline.
- The story of Samson serves as a mirror in which we can see ourselves as we really are.

REFLECTION & DISCUSSION QUESTIONS

🕐 Before the Video

What Do You Think?

- What do you already know about Samson? What do you think of his story?
- Why are you undertaking this study of Samson? What do you hope to get out of it?

Scripture Reading

And what more shall I say? For time would fail me to tell of Gideon, Barak, Samson, Jephthah, of David and Samuel and the prophets—who through faith conquered kingdoms, enforced justice, obtained promises, stopped the mouths of lions, quenched the power of fire, escaped the edge of the sword, were made strong out of weakness, became mighty in war, put foreign armies to flight.... And all these, though commended through their faith, did not receive what was promised.

—Hebrews 11:32–34, 39

- What does this passage tell us about Samson? How does it assess his life?

🕐 During the Video

▶ *Play the video; pause at 12:57.*

What Samson Teaches Us

- How is Samson both a mirror and a riddle?
- Dr. Godfrey highlights three lessons we will learn from this study of Samson. Summarize in your own words what Dr. Godfrey intends to address in these lessons.
    Spiritual failures
    Relevance to Christ
    Importance of context

▶ *Play the video to the end.*

The Context of the Story

- How many judges does Dr. Godfrey see in the book of Judges? What is the significance of this number?
- Who are the two most prominent judges in the book of Judges? What makes them the most important?
- The book of Judges is not a comprehensive survey of all of Israel's judges but a series of snapshots that communicate a particular message. What is that message?

🕐 After the Video

- How does the book of Judges point to Christ? How is this made especially clear in the stories of the best judge, Deborah, and the worst judge, Samson?

    If you are in a group, read together the account of Deborah in Judges 4–5. Then, work together to create a list of the qualities that marked Deborah as a good judge. Save this list and be prepared to return to it in lesson 7, "The Foolishness of Samson."

- Hebrews commends Samson for his faith and mighty deeds (Heb. 11:32–40), yet the story of Samson in Judges portrays him not as a savior of Israel but as Israel itself in all its spiritual failings. How can Samson be both a failure and faithful?

  If you are in a group, have the members name Samson's memorable acts and discuss whether each is evidence of faith or failure.

- What are the two most important concepts you learned in this lesson? Why did these stand out to you? How do you think these concepts will affect the way you see Samson's story?

  If you are in a group, have each member identify one or two concepts that were most outstanding to them and discuss their significance together.

PRAYER

- Praise God for the sovereignty and love He displays in His care for His people.
- Confess your frequent unreceptiveness to God as He speaks through His Word.
- Thank God for His gift of Christ, the perfect Judge to whom Israel's judges pointed.
- Ask God to cause you to take to heart the lessons He has for you from the life of Samson.

REVIEW QUIZ

1. Dr. Godfrey highlighted a few reasons why it is valuable to study the life of Samson. Which of the following is *not* one of those reasons?
   a. It is a story that points us to Christ.
   b. It is a story that helps us see how to study the Bible properly.
   c. It is a story that helps us see the salvation of Israel.
   d. It is a story that warns about spiritual failures to avoid.

2. Which of these leaders in the book of Judges was not actually a judge?
   a. Gideon
   b. Deborah
   c. Samson
   d. Barak

3. Which of these judges in the book of Judges was closest to a perfect judge?
   a. Deborah
   b. Othniel
   c. Gideon
   d. Ehud

4. How many judges are discussed in the book of Judges?
   a. 12
   b. 13
   c. 6
   d. 7

5. The book of Judges provides us with a comprehensive history of the period from Joshua to Saul.
   a. True
   b. False

6. Which of the following statements best summarizes the spiritual trajectory of the judges?
   a. With exceptions, they tended to represent the worst of Israel's sinfulness.
   b. Each subsequent judge experienced greater longevity and blessing.
   c. The judges followed the decline of Israel, experiencing shorter and shorter reigns and less and less blessing.
   d. The faithfulness of the judges is sporadic; there is no pattern of spiritual decline.

Answer Key—The Riddle of Samson

REFLECTION & DISCUSSION QUESTIONS

🕐 Before the Video

What Do You Think?

> *These are personal questions. The answers should be based on your own knowledge and experience.*

Scripture Reading

- What does this passage tell us about Samson? What is this assessment of his life?

  This passage tells us that Samson, despite what we know (or will learn) about him from the book of Judges, is commendable on account of his faith. That faith, furthermore, is evident in his actions.

🕐 During the Video

What Samson Teaches Us

- How is Samson both a mirror and a riddle?

  Samson is a mirror in that through him we can see ourselves as we truly are. Samson is also a riddle since we know from Scripture that he was a man of great sin and great faith. The key to understanding Samson's story is to see how both of these can be true of the same person.

- Dr. Godfrey highlights three lessons we will learn from this study of Samson. Summarize in your own words what Dr. Godfrey intends to address in these lessons.

  Spiritual failures: The story of Samson is a series of warnings about spiritual failures to avoid. One of the main lessons we learn from Samson is what not to do.

  Relevance to Christ: Samson and the rest of Israel's judges point to Christ. They are imperfect saviors of Israel who highlight the need for the only perfect Judge/Savior, Christ Himself.

  Importance of context: This series will examine the story of Samson in the context of the whole of Scripture (the big picture) and the specific context of Samson in the book of Judges. Both contexts are necessary for Bible study and to learn the lessons God has for us in the life of Samson.

The Context of the Story

- How many judges does Dr. Godfrey see in the book of Judges? What is the significance of this number?

Dr. Godfrey identifies twelve judges, although he admits that the precise number is debated among scholars. He argues that this number is supported by the evidence of the biblical record and is likely given the significance of the number twelve. It represents the tribes of Israel and therefore speaks to both the composition of God's people and how God relates to His people.

- Who are the two most prominent judges in the book of Judges? What makes them the most important?

  Gideon and Samson are the two most prominent judges. They are given the closest and longest attention of any of the judges. Also, their stories are the most complex and mixed in terms of the lessons they teach.

- The book of Judges is not a comprehensive survey of all of Israel's judges but a series of snapshots that communicate a particular message. What is that message?

  In the book of Judges, God is giving us a series of snapshots that show the spiritual decline of Israel. The diminishing reigns and shrinking families of the judges reflect the gradual reduction in Israel's blessing.

🕐 After the Video

- How does the book of Judges point to Christ? How is this made especially clear in the stories of the best judge, Deborah, and the worst judge, Samson?

  The judges are imperfect and therefore insufficient saviors of Israel. The book of Judges makes it clear that Israel needs a perfect and all-powerful Savior. Samson is the culminating judge, the picture of how far Israel had fallen and how incapable human judges were to save the nation. Even Deborah, the best judge (who was too good to be used as an example of God's weak and needy leaders in Hebrews), could not save God's people.

- Hebrews commends Samson for his faith and mighty deeds (Heb. 11:32–40), yet the story of Samson in Judges portrays him not as a savior of Israel but as Israel itself in all its spiritual failings. How can Samson be both a failure and faithful?

  Samson's spiritual failures and faithfulness are not mutually exclusive. The book of Judges shows us the specific context of Samson's largely dishonorable and disappointing life. The letter to the Hebrews shows us the bigger picture of Samson's significance in light of how God used him.

- What are the two most important concepts you learned in this lesson? Why did these stand out to you? How do you think these concepts will affect the way you see Samson's story?

  The answers to these questions should express what you considered the most outstanding and personally relevant lessons from this lecture.

REVIEW QUIZ

1. **C.**

   All of the judges in the book of Judges were appointed to save Israel, including Samson. But Samson doesn't represent a savior of Israel; he is Israel. His life reveals all the weaknesses and spiritual failures of the nation. In this way, Samson's story points to Christ, the only perfect Judge and Savior.

2. **D.**

   Barak is a prominent figure in Judges, but he was not a judge himself. He served in a supporting role to Deborah, who was the real judge at the time.

3. **A.**

   While Othniel, Ehud, and Deborah were all very positive judges, Deborah most closely portrays a perfect judge. When the fathers in Israel failed, God raised up a mother in Israel to lead them. Of course, she was not perfect. Deborah, like the rest, points to the need for the truly perfect Judge, Christ Himself.

4. **A.**

   While the book of Judges is not exhaustive in its coverage of Israel's judges, it does address twelve of them. However, we're only given significant detail about six of them, the "major judges": Othniel, Ehud, Deborah, Gideon, Jephthah, and Samson.

5. **B.**

   Rather than an exhaustive history of this period, Judges provides a series of snapshots to trace the spiritual decline—and suffering—of Israel. It also focuses only on specific areas, since the judges ruled regionally rather than covering the whole country.

6. **C.**

   The general spiritual trajectory of the judges is decline. Whereas the earlier major judges ruled forty years, the last three minor judges ruled less than ten years each, reflecting a decrease in God's blessing. The spiritual decline of the judges followed the spiritual decline of Israel as a whole.

2

The Need for Judges

INTRODUCTION

God instituted the office of judge to help Israel in her state of spiritual decline. Israel's continued decline even during this period reveals the intent behind the book of Judges, which functions as a treatise on Israel's need for a king. In this lesson, Dr. Godfrey places the book of Judges within its context in the Bible to further develop our understanding of the book's final judge, Samson.

LEARNING GOALS

When you have finished this lesson, you should be able to:

- Trace the narrative line of the Bible from Joshua through Judges to Ruth
- Identify the overall pattern in which God reveals His steadfast love in Scripture

KEY IDEAS

- The story of Israel's failure in the period of the judges anticipates Israel's need for a king.
- Judges forms a cohesive narrative within its biblical context between Joshua and Ruth.
- Israel's pattern of struggle throughout Scripture is the stage on which God reveals His love to us in Jesus Christ, who conquers both our sin and our enemies as King.

REFLECTION & DISCUSSION QUESTIONS

🕐 Before the Video

What Do You Think?

- From what you know about the book of Judges, how would you summarize its message and purpose within the Bible?

- What relevance do the message and purpose of Judges have for the church today?

Scripture Reading

When you come to the land that the Lord *your God is giving you, and you possess it and dwell in it and then say, "I will set a king over me, like all the nations that are around me," you may indeed set a king over you whom the* Lord *your God will choose. . . .*

 And when he sits on the throne of his kingdom, he shall write for himself in a book a copy of this law, approved by the Levitical priests. And it shall be with him, and he shall read in it all the days of his life, that he may learn to fear the Lord *his God by keeping all the words of this law and these statutes, and doing them.*

              —Deuteronomy 17:14–15, 18–19

- What does God's law require of Israel's kings? How does this foreshadow Jesus Christ?

🕐 During the Video

▶ *Play the video; pause at 14:50.*

The Narrative Features of Judges

- How does the book of Judges continue the theme established at the end of Joshua?
- How does the book of Judges form a cohesive narrative with the book of Ruth? In particular, how does the book of Judges function as an argument against the kingship of Saul?

▶ *Play the video to the end.*

The Struggles of Israel

- What is significant about the fact that God maintains His promise of salvation throughout Israel's struggles in the Old Testament?
- What do the similarities between Israel's struggles in the Old Testament and the church's struggles in the New Testament teach us about the nature of sanctification?
- How should Psalm 85 inform our prayers for ourselves and for our country?

🕐 After the Video

- "Everyone did what was right in his own eyes" is a refrain found throughout the book of Judges. How does this refrain underline the rhetorical purpose of the book of Judges?

  If you are in a group, read together the partial account of Samson's marriage in Judges 14:1–7. Identify which verses allude to this refrain and discuss what they may reveal about Samson as a judge in Israel.

- Why is it important to read the book of Judges in light of the books that come before and after it?

  If you are in a group, discuss other places in Scripture where you have seen the value of reading a passage or book in its context. How does this affect your view of Scripture?

- How has the pattern of spiritual struggle that Dr. Godfrey highlighted in Psalm 85 been confirmed by your own experience? Does this make you hopeful or frustrated? Why?

  If you are in a group, share with one another what passages of Scripture have been most helpful in your spiritual struggles.

PRAYER

- Praise God for His knowledge and wisdom in directing the course of human history.
- Confess any stubborn and half-hearted repentance that currently exists in your life.
- Thank God that He loves you and that His promises are extended to you even when you sin.
- Ask God to help you further recognize your sin through the power of the Holy Spirit so that you might grow in holiness for His name's sake.

REVIEW QUIZ

1. In the last chapter of Joshua, Joshua told Israel, "You are not able to serve the LORD." What was Dr. Godfrey's interpretation of Joshua's statement?
   a. Joshua was expressing Israel's merely human inability to serve a holy God.
   b. Joshua was constructing an argument that would incline Israel's heart to God.
   c. Joshua had foreseen that Israel would fall into the sin of idolatry against God.
   d. Joshua had anticipated Israel's need for a faithful leader in order to serve God.

2. What book of the Bible focuses on the story behind the lineage of David?
   a. Ruth
   b. 1 Samuel
   c. 2 Samuel
   d. 1 Kings

3. When was the book of Judges likely to have been compiled into its final form?
   a. During the reign of Saul
   b. During the reign of David
   c. During the period of the judges
   d. During the period of the patriarchs

4. What city is highlighted in Judges to function as an argument against Saul as a king?
    a. Bethel
    b. Gibeah
    c. Shechem
    d. Jerusalem

5. We should not view the judges in Israel's history as playing a primarily judicial role.
    a. True
    b. False

6. What spiritual pattern in which God interacts with His people does Psalm 85 follow?
    a. An upward pattern of constant victory
    b. A downward pattern of uncertain doubt
    c. An up-and-down pattern of spiritual struggle
    d. An up-and-down pattern of half-hearted faith

Answer Key—The Need for Judges

🕐 Before the Video

What Do You Think?

These are personal questions. The answers should be based on your own knowledge and experience.

Scripture Reading

- What does God's law require of Israel's kings? How does this foreshadow Jesus Christ?

  The larger context of this passage reveals to us a number of God's laws for an Israelite king. Here, we can see that the only acceptable king in Israel is one who is chosen by God and who, furthermore, lives by the standard of God's law. This passage foreshadows Jesus Christ, as He alone has fulfilled perfectly the law of God as the chosen King of kings and Lord of lords.

🕐 During the Video

The Narrative Features of Judges

- How does the book of Judges continue the theme established at the end of Joshua?

  The theme established in the last chapter of the book of Joshua is Israel's need of faithful leadership in order to maintain God's standard of righteousness as revealed in His law. From Joshua's last words, the people of Israel are being prepared for their need of a king. Thus, the book of Judges serves as a transitional book from Joshua into the historical narratives about the kings of Israel.

- How does the book of Judges form a cohesive narrative with the book of Ruth? In particular, how does the book of Judges function as a polemic against the kingship of Saul?

  The book of Judges points to Israel's need for a king, but not just any king—a king chosen by God from the tribe of Judah. It is here that we can begin to see the book of Judges as a polemic against the kingship of Saul in the way it contrasts the tribe of Judah and the tribe of Benjamin, especially in highlighting the tribe of Benjamin's sin at Gibeah. The book of Ruth continues this narrative by narrowing its focus on David's lineage.

The Struggles of Israel

- What is significant about the fact that God maintains His promise of salvation throughout Israel's struggles in the Old Testament?

  God's promises to His people are especially significant during periods of difficulty, for it is the pattern revealed in Scripture by which God unveils His love to us. He is faithful to His promises even in our failures. This is as true for us as it was for Israel, from whom God never withheld His promises—all the more reason for us to worship and obey Him.

- What do the similarities between Israel's struggles in the Old Testament and the church's struggles in the New Testament teach us about the nature of sanctification?

  Israel's struggle in the Old Testament is widely applicable to our Christian experience. As can be seen in the letters of the New Testament, the Apostles wrote to address various needs and struggles of Christians, who though having been set apart were not yet perfect. This teaches us that there is a progressive dimension to sanctification.

- How should Psalm 85 inform our prayers for ourselves and for our country?

  Psalm 85 fundamentally directs us to pray prayers of repentance, trusting that God will revive us again. Such prayers can be extended beyond our personal context to the cultural and national level, helping us to pray earnestly with heartfelt concern for the needs of our country, that the grace of Jesus Christ might be known far and wide.

⏱ After the Video

- "Everyone did what was right in his own eyes" is a refrain found throughout the book of Judges. How does this refrain underline the rhetorical purpose of the book of Judges?

  The book of Judges sets out to showcase the sinful imperfections of the leaders in Israel, which underscored Israel's need for a faithful leader. Ultimately, Israel needed a king. This is the reason that people did what was right in their own eyes, because "in those days there was no king in Israel" (Judg. 17:6; 21:25).

- Why is it important to read the book of Judges in light of the book that comes before it—Joshua—and the book that comes after it—Ruth?

  Reading the book of Judges contextually is important because the Bible isn't a collection of isolated stories that do not relate to one another. Rather, the Bible is a cohesive story, so just as the book of Joshua ends with a question about leadership in Israel, the book of Judges carries along the story line about Israel's unfaithful leaders, pointing to Israel's need for a king—a king whose lineage is taken up in the book of Ruth. All this is found within the even greater narrative of our King, Jesus Christ.

- How has the pattern of spiritual struggle that Dr. Godfrey highlighted in Psalm 85 been confirmed by your own experience? Does this make you hopeful or frustrated? Why?

  The answers to these questions should take into consideration both Psalm 85 and your personal experience and growth in grace. Consider how you emotionally process sin alongside the promises that you have in Christ.

REVIEW QUIZ

1. **D.**

   Dr. Godfrey interpreted Joshua's statement "You are not able to serve the Lord" in terms of Joshua's concern for a leaderless Israel. Joshua understood that Israel would need a faithful leader in order to serve the Lord, and the leadership of Israel was not being given to another singly appointed leader, as was the case when God appointed Joshua to lead Israel after Moses.

2. **A.**

   The book of Ruth focuses on the story behind David's lineage. Since the book of Judges highlights Israel's need for a faithful king, the canonical order of Ruth after the book of Judges significantly draws our attention to the cohesive narrative of the Bible.

3. **B.**

   Because of how the tribe of Judah and the tribe of Benjamin are so heavily contrasted in the book of Judges, it is most likely that the book of Judges was compiled into its final form during the reign of David, God's appointed king from the tribe of Judah. Seen in this light, the book of Judges is a divinely inspired tract for the house of David.

4. **B.**

   Judges 19:22–30 recounts the tribe of Benjamin's horrific sin in the city of Gibeah, and Saul is from the tribe of Benjamin and the city of Gibeah. Thus, this story paints Saul's kingship in a negative light, foreshadowing his failures.

5. **A.**

   The judges throughout Israel's history were not judges in a judicial sense, which is how we typically think of judges within a modern-day court system. Rather, the judges in Israel were leaders who primarily made decisions for the people, leading them against their sins and their enemies. In this sense, the judges of Israel prefigured Christ.

6. **C.**

   Psalm 85 is a wonderful example of how God meets His people in their spiritual need, through the everyday ups and downs of confession, repentance, and faith. These things mark the Christian life, and as we pursue holiness, it isn't always easy. That's why the pattern of ups and downs in Psalm 85 is so reassuring, as it helps us look to the steadfast love of the Lord through our spiritual struggles.

3

The Need for Samson

INTRODUCTION

Just as Israel's need for the office of judge pointed to Israel's need for a king, so Israel's need for Samson pointed to an even greater spiritual need. In this lesson, Dr. Godfrey highlights the major themes in Samson's story, allowing us to see the story's big picture while at the same time focusing our attention on the story's opening scene.

LEARNING GOALS

When you have finished this lesson, you should be able to:

- Describe the spiritual climate in Israel during the era of the judges
- Divide the story of Samson into its parts
- Comprehend how God intends us to see Samson

KEY IDEAS

- Idolatry was Israel's major struggle upon entering the Promised Land.
- Samson's story can be divided into four main acts, the first of which introduces us to Samson's parents and recounts his miraculous birth.

REFLECTION & DISCUSSION QUESTIONS

🕐 Before the Video

What Do You Think?

- What sins does God consider to be most offensive? Why?
- How many events had to come together for you to have even been born? What does this say about God and the nature of the world?

Scripture Reading

> *But just as all the good things that the Lord your God promised concerning you have been fulfilled for you, so the Lord will bring upon you all the evil things, until he has destroyed you from off this good land that the Lord your God has given you, if you transgress the covenant of the Lord your God, which he commanded you, and go and serve other gods and bow down to them.*
>
> —Joshua 23:15–16

- What is revealed to be the fundamental violation of God's covenant in this passage? What punishment would God bring upon Israel for such a violation?

🕐 During the Video

▶ *Play the video; pause at 9:01.*

Israel's Idolatry

- In Judges 10, which is the most detailed statement of Israel's unfaithfulness in the book of Judges, what is significant about the list of gods that Israel worshiped?
- What was the punishment for Israel's idolatry before God raised up Samson?

▶ *Play the video to the end.*

Samson's Parents & Birth

- In what way are Samson's parents representative of the overall character of Israel during the period before God raised up Samson?
- Why was barrenness seen to be a curse from the Lord in Israel?
- What instructions for her son did Samson's mother receive from the angel of the Lord?

🕐 After the Video

- Numbers 33:55 clearly states that the people of Canaan would become thorns in Israel's side if they were not driven out from the land. In what ways did the people of Canaan prove to be thorns in Israel's side during the period of the judges?

  If you are in a group, discuss various objects of idolatry that exist in our day. How are they different from the objects of Israel's idolatry? How are they similar?

- What was the primary role of the angel of the Lord in the story of Samson's birth? Who do many conservative scholars consider the angel of the Lord to be?

  If you are in a group, compare Samson's birth with other miraculous births in the Bible such as those of John the Baptist, Samuel, or Jesus. What similarities or dissimilarities can you find between them?

- How does the fact that Samson was a Nazirite from his mother's womb inform us of how God intended Samson to be viewed?

  If you are in a group, read Numbers 6 together. Can you draw out any principles from the Nazirite vow that can be applied to the life of every Christian?

PRAYER

- Praise God as the one living and true God.
- Confess any idols of the heart that prevent you from worshiping Him alone.
- Thank God for giving you the gift of life and the gift of faith.
- Ask God to use you to direct others to worship Him.

REVIEW QUIZ

1. What theme did Dr. Godfrey introduce as important to Samson's story, especially in terms of the perspective of the Lord?
   a. The theme of sight
   b. The theme of idolatry
   c. The theme of strength
   d. The theme of barrenness

2. What was the particularly evil sin that Israel committed during the period of the judges?
   a. Israel married foreign wives.
   b. Israel created images of the Lord.
   c. Israel tolerated the people of Canaan.
   d. Israel worshiped images of false gods.

3. What is likely alluded to in Israel's forty-year oppression under the Philistines?
   a. The forty days Moses spent on Mount Sinai
   b. The forty years Israel spent in the wilderness
   c. The forty days Israel spent spying out the land of Canaan
   d. The forty years Moses spent in Midian before returning to Egypt

4. How much of Samson's story is devoted to his parents and birth?
   a. 10 percent
   b. 15 percent
   c. 25 percent
   d. 35 percent

5. Delilah is the only woman who is known by name in Samson's story.
   a. True
   b. False

6. What is the most fundamental part of the Nazirite vow?
   a. Abstinence from all wine and strong drink
   b. Caution against any uncleanness
   c. Commitment to never cut one's hair
   d. Separation of oneself to the Lord

Answer Key—The Need for Samson

🕐 Before the Video

What Do You Think?

> *These are personal questions. The answers should be based on your own knowledge and experience.*

Scripture Reading

- What is revealed to be the fundamental violation of God's covenant in this passage? What punishment would God bring upon Israel for such a violation?

  This passage reveals that the fundamental violation of God's covenant is idolatry, which was Israel's primary struggle among the nations. God promised to punish such idolatry by expelling the people from the land, which came to pass in the Babylonian exile.

🕐 During the Video

Israel's Idolatry

- In Judges 10, which is the most detailed statement of Israel's unfaithfulness in the book of Judges, what is significant about the gods that Israel worshiped?

  The gods listed in Judges 10 are the gods of the people surrounding Israel in the Promised Land. It is significant that particular gods and people groups are mentioned, because this indicates the extent of Israel's idolatry. Israel worshiped gods in every direction—north, south, east, and west.

- What was the punishment for Israel's idolatry before God raised up Samson?

  Israel's idolatry resulted in forty years of slavery and oppression at the hands of the Philistines. This is the context in which God raised up Samson to deliver His people.

Samson's Parents & Birth

- In what way are Samson's parents representative of the overall character of Israel during the period before God raised up Samson?

  Unlike Hannah, who fervently prayed for a child while barren, Samson's mother seems to have been resigned to never having a child. In this story, we are never told that Samson's parents cried out to the Lord for help, but God visited them nonetheless. Here, Samson's parents are representative of Israel's overall hopelessness after forty years of Philistine rule.

- Why was barrenness seen to be a curse from the Lord in Israel?

  In Israel, barrenness was seen to be a curse from the Lord because without children a family line could not continue and was in jeopardy of dying out entirely. In a profound way, this related to God's promise of the Messiah who would be born from Israel. Thus, barrenness threatened more than the continuation of tribal or familial lines; it threatened salvation itself.

- What instructions for her son did Samson's mother receive from the angel of the Lord?

  Samson's mother received instructions that Samson was to be a Nazirite from the womb. Therefore, she was not to drink any wine or strong drink or eat any unclean food. Samson was likewise to continue these obligations, and he was never to cut his hair. For a fuller treatment of the laws of a Nazirite, refer to Numbers 6.

⏱ After the Video

- Numbers 33:55 clearly states that the people of Canaan would become thorns in Israel's side if they were not driven out from the land. In what ways did the people of Canaan prove to be thorns in Israel's side during the period of the judges?

  The warning of Numbers 33:55 came to pass for Israel because they did not drive out the people of Canaan from the land. As a result, these people became thorns in Israel's side because Israel would worship their gods and God would subsequently discipline Israel with the very people with whom Israel fell into idolatry. We clearly see this in Judges 13:1 when God gave Israel into the hands of the Philistines for forty years as punishment for idolatry.

- What was the primary role of the angel of the Lord in the story of Samson's birth? Who do many conservative scholars consider the angel of the Lord to be?

  The angel of the Lord in the story of Samson's birth is primarily fulfilling the role of a messenger. Both the Hebrew and the Greek words for "angel" mean "messenger," so angels fundamentally deliver a word from God. Many conservative scholars consider manifestations of the angel of the Lord in the Old Testament to be preincarnate appearances of Christ.

- How does the fact that Samson was a Nazirite from his mother's womb inform us of how God intended Samson to be viewed?

  "Nazirite" is a Hebrew word that means "separated," so the fact that Samson was a Nazirite from his mother's womb indicates that God intended for Samson to be viewed as an individual consecrated for the Lord. This was a lesson Israel desperately needed to learn, that they were to be set apart for the Lord in their life and worship.

REVIEW QUIZ

1. **A.**

    All of these choices can be considered thematic in Samson's story, but Dr. Godfrey cited the theme of sight as particularly important. The theme is introduced in the very first verse of Judges 13, the chapter that begins Samson's story. In Judges 13:1, our attention is drawn to Israel's idolatry, which was "evil in the sight of the Lord."

2. **D.**

    Before the period of the judges, Israel had worshiped graven images of the Lord, such as in the golden calf incident of Exodus 32. In the period of the judges however, Israel had fallen to such an extent that they worshiped images of false gods, an even greater offense to the one true God of Israel.

3. **B.**

    The forty years of oppression that Israel faced at the hands of the Philistines was a sign of just how far Israel had fallen. The fact that it was a forty-year period of sub-jugation alludes to the forty years that Israel wandered in the wilderness. Although Israel had been given the Promised Land, it was almost as if they had never entered it and were still wandering in the wilderness as a result of their idolatry.

4. **C.**

    Twenty-five percent of Samson's story is devoted to his parents and birth, indicating the importance of this portion of his story in shaping how God really wants us to think about Samson, his context, and the task that was given to him. This is significant considering that the third act of Samson's story is a mere three verses.

5. **A.**

    Women play a significant role in Samson's story, yet in the first three acts of his story the women are not named, even including Samson's pious mother. The only woman in the story who is known by name is found in the fourth act—Delilah, the Philistine woman famous for bringing about Samson's downfall.

6. **D.**

    "Nazirite" is a Hebrew word that means "separated," so the most fundamental part of the Nazirite vow is not the various laws that make up the vow, but to what those laws point, that is, the separation of oneself to the Lord.

4

The Promise of Samson

INTRODUCTION

When we think of Samson, first and foremost, we need to think of him as one set apart unto the Lord. Samson's renowned strength can only be secondary to the call of holiness upon his life. In this lesson, Dr. Godfrey creates a character sketch of Samson's parents upon their receiving the promise of his birth and outlines the express instruction they received to consecrate him to the Lord.

LEARNING GOALS

When you have finished this lesson, you should be able to:
- Recount the faithful acts of Samson's parents in Judges 13
- Identify the role played by the angel of the Lord in Judges 13
- Understand the tension introduced by act 2 of Samson's story

KEY IDEAS

- The piety of Samson's parents before the angel of the Lord points to the faithful manner in which they would raise Samson as a Nazirite.
- The angel of the Lord in act 1 of Samson's story is a preincarnate manifestation of Christ, who pictures the degree to which Samson is to be consecrated to God.
- Act 2 of Samson's story sharply contrasts act 1 of Samson's story.

REFLECTION & DISCUSSION QUESTIONS

🕐 Before the Video

What Do You Think?

- What role did your parents play in shaping your faith?
- How do people typically react to encounters with God in the Bible? What do these divine encounters teach you about God?

Scripture Reading

So Manoah took the young goat with the grain offering, and offered it on the rock to the LORD, *to the one who works wonders, and Manoah and his wife were watching. And when the flame went up toward heaven from the altar, the angel of the* LORD *went up in the flame of the altar. Now Manoah and his wife were watching, and they fell on their faces to the ground.*

—Judges 13:19–20

- This passage beautifully refers to God as "the one who works wonders." What wondrous work did God promise to do in the life of Manoah and his wife? How did they respond?

🕐 During the Video

▶️ *Play the video; pause at 14:34.*

The Angel of the Lord

- How did the angel of the Lord depart from Samson's parents? Why is this significant?
- What was the immediate reaction of Samson's parents when the angel of the Lord departed from them? What did they think would happen to them?
- In light of our privileges as Christians, what important lesson do Samson's parents and their reaction to the angel of the Lord teach us?

▶️ *Play the video to the end.*

Samson's Philistine Wife

- In what way does the beginning of act 2 of Samson's story sharply contrast with act 1?
- Should it even matter who Samson wanted to marry? Why was his desire for a Philistine wife more of a problem than if he had desired an Israelite?

🕐 After the Video

- What does Dr. Godfrey consider to be a great temptation for Christians related to the desire for their children's success?

  If you are in a group, have the members share what they consider to be the most significant instructions the Bible gives for raising children.

- Dr. Godfrey has highlighted the piety of Samson's parents throughout this lecture. In what way did Manoah and his wife fail in their responsibility as parents?

If you are in a group, have the members name the most memorable demonstrations of piety by Samson's parents in their encounters with the angel of the Lord.

- Did Samson's desire for a Philistine wife jeopardize God's plan to use Samson to deliver Israel? How do you know?

If you are in a group, discuss the relationship of God's sovereignty and man's responsibility. What does Samson's story tell you about this relationship?

PRAYER

- Praise God for His radiant holiness and inapproachable majesty.
- Confess ways in which you have presumed upon God's mercy.
- Thank God for granting you access to Him as a loving Father.
- Ask God to bless you with a deeper reverence for Him.

REVIEW QUIZ

1. What literary device is used for emphasis in the story of Samson's parents?
   a. Imagery
   b. Allusion
   c. Metaphor
   d. Repetition

2. The offering of Samson's parents parallels the offering made by which judge?
   a. Deborah
   b. Othniel
   c. Gideon
   d. Ehud

3. What common theme links together each of the major acts of Samson's story?
   a. Samson's defeat of the Philistines
   b. Samson's staggering feats of strength
   c. Samson's failure to keep the Nazirite vow
   d. Samson's relationship with different women

4. What Old Testament story did Dr. Godfrey use to illustrate God's ability to sovereignly use Samson despite his sin?
   a. The story of Jacob's being blessed by Isaac
   b. The story of Pharaoh's being hardened by God
   c. The story of Joseph's being sold into slavery by his brothers
   d. The story of Cyrus' being used as an instrument of judgment against Israel

5. The angel of the Lord told Manoah and his wife what to name their child.
   a. True
   b. False

6. What word is Samson's name related to in the original Hebrew?
   a. Sin
   b. Sun
   c. Sorrow
   d. Strength

Answer Key—The Promise of Samson

🕐 Before the Video

What Do You Think?

These are personal questions. The answers should be based on your own knowledge and experience.

Scripture Reading

- This passage beautifully refers to God as "the one who works wonders." What wondrous work did God promise to do in the life of Manoah and his wife? How did they respond?

  God promised to bless Manoah and his wife in their barrenness by giving them a son, Samson. They responded to the promise of his birth by making an offering to God.

🕐 During the Video

The Angel of the Lord

- How did the angel of the Lord depart from Samson's parents? Why is this significant?

  The angel of the Lord departed from Samson's parents by being consumed in the flame of the burnt offering. This is significant for two reasons. First, it pictures the extent to which Samson is to be consecrated to God. Second, it pictures the loving sacrifice of Christ for our atonement on the cross.

- What was the immediate reaction of Samson's parents when the angel of the Lord departed from them? What did they think would happen to them?

  After the angel of the Lord departed, Samson's parents immediately fell upon their faces in a posture of worship and reverential fear. Furthermore, Manoah was fearful that they were going to die for having seen God (Judg. 13:22). Manoah's wife understood that, though they had seen God, the promise would be fulfilled.

- In light of our privileges as Christians, what important lesson do Samson's parents and their reaction to the angel of the Lord teach us?

  As Christians, we have the incredible privilege of addressing God as "Father" and can freely come before Him in Christ. Samson's parents and their reaction to the angel of the Lord teach us how serious it is to come before God, so that we might not presume upon His kindness to us as our Father.

Samson's Philistine Wife

- In what way does the beginning of act 2 of Samson's story sharply contrast with act 1?

  Act 1 teaches how we should think about Samson as one consecrated to the Lord, as it even ends with a description of the way God blessed Samson as he matured. Act 2 sharply contrasts with act 1 by narrating Samson's desire for a Philistine bride, a bride from the very ones who ruled over Israel.

- Should it even matter who Samson wanted to marry? Why is his desire for a Philistine wife more of a problem than if he had desired an Israelite?

  First and foremost, Samson's desire for a Philistine wife and the consummation of that desire was a violation of God's law. God warned the Israelites against intermarriage with those who worshiped other gods because they would lure Israel away from serving the one true God. In the end, a Philistine woman would be Samson's great downfall.

⏱ After the Video

- What does Dr. Godfrey consider to be a great temptation for Christians related to the desire for their children's success?

  A great temptation for Christians who have a desire for their children's success is not the desire for success itself, which is a right and good desire, but rather for their children's success both before God and before the world. This temptation could cause parents to settle for and be content with their children's merely worldly success.

- Dr. Godfrey has highlighted the piety of Samson's parents throughout this lecture. In what way did Manoah and his wife fail in their responsibility as parents?

  Samson's parents failed in their responsibility by facilitating Samson's marriage to a Philistine woman. This action was in direct conflict with their commission to raise Samson as one consecrated to the Lord.

- Did Samson's desire for a Philistine wife jeopardize God's plan to use Samson to deliver Israel? How do you know?

  Samson's desire for a Philistine wife in no way jeopardized God's plan to use Samson to deliver Israel from the Philistines. We know that God is sovereign, and His will can be thwarted by no man. Therefore, God could use Samson in spite of and through his sin. Perhaps the most important reason we know that God's plan was not in jeopardy is that Scripture clearly tells us (Judg. 14:4).

REVIEW QUIZ

1. **D.**

   Repetition is the literary device used for emphasis in the story of Samson's parents. Repetition is intended to draw our attention to the important points of a story. In the encounters of Samson's parents with the angel of the Lord, the angel repeats three times what he says concerning Samson's consecration to God.

2. **C.**

   The offering of Samson's parents in Judges 13 parallels the offering made by Gideon in Judges 6. Both accounts involve an offering made in the presence of the angel of the Lord, yet there is a significant difference in the manner in which the angel of the Lord departs from Gideon and the manner in which he departs from Samson's parents.

3. **D.**

   The various acts of Samson's story are linked together by a common theme: Samson's relationship with women. From Samson's mother to Delilah, the acts in his story correspond to his relationships with different women. After the story of Samson's mother, Samson's relationship with women is particularly shocking because of his involvement with various Philistine women.

4. **C.**

   Dr. Godfrey used the account of Joseph's being sold into slavery to illustrate how God can use men despite their sin to accomplish His purposes. Just as Samson's parents were not aware that Samson's marriage to a Philistine woman would be used by God, Joseph's brothers were not aware that their evil would be used by God for good (Gen. 50:20).

5. **B.**

   The angel of the Lord did not tell Manoah and his wife what to name their child. They named him Samson freely. This places a considerable emphasis on the one thing the angel of the Lord did tell Samson's parents, which was to consecrate him to the Lord.

6. **B.**

   Samson's name is related to the Hebrew word for "sun," which gives us a vivid picture of what Manoah and his wife thought about God's gift to them. By naming their son Samson, they demonstrated how brightly their son shined upon them in a very dark time in the history of Israel.

5

The Selfishness of Samson

INTRODUCTION

Samson's choice of a wife was characterized by self-indulgence. He walked by sight and not by faith, yet God still used him as a judge in Israel. In this lesson, Dr. Godfrey demonstrates how Samson's selfishness led to dark and violent episodes of tyranny and revenge.

LEARNING GOALS

When you have finished this lesson, you should be able to:
- Recognize the ultimate source of Samson's strength
- Identify the dire consequences of Samson's selfishness
- Trace the theme of violence through act 2 of Samson's story

KEY IDEAS

- Samson's strength was meant to be a sign of the presence of God's Spirit in his life.
- God intervened in Samson's life through an encounter with a lion, yet Samson failed to see the spiritual implications of the encounter and the riddle inspired by the encounter.
- Samson used the strength that God had given him for violent self-indulgence.

REFLECTION & DISCUSSION QUESTIONS

🕐 Before the Video

What Do You Think?

- How has your perspective on Samson changed since beginning this study?
- How has God exposed to you the folly of your ways in order to preserve you from

the full repercussions of your sin?

- Do you consider violence to be fundamentally evil? Can it ever be used for good, right, and necessary ends? Why or why not?

Scripture Reading

Do not love the world or things in the world. If anyone loves the world, the love of the Father is not in him. For all that is in the world—the desires of the flesh and the desires of the eyes and the pride of life—is not from the Father but is from the world.

—1 John 2:15–16

- How has Samson thus far demonstrated the qualities of someone who loves the world?

🕐 During the Video

▶ *Play the video; pause at 13:53.*

Samson's Riddle

- What was the riddle that Samson put to the Philistines?
- What lesson may God have been teaching Samson from his experience with the lion? What truth did Samson miss from his very own riddle?

▶ *Play the video to the end.*

The Viciousness of Sin

- What was the wager of Samson's riddle? Was it a significant wager? Why?
- How does violence escalate in act 2 of Samson's story?
- How does the end of this lesson suggest that a cycle of violence and revenge will continue in the remainder of act 2 in Samson's story?

🕐 After the Video

- How was Samson able to defeat the lion on his journey to the marriage feast?

  If you are in a group, discuss other accounts where men encountered lions in the Bible. Read 1 Samuel 17:31–37 and Daniel 6:16–24. What do these stories have in common? Consider that the devil is described as a roaring lion in 1 Peter 5:8. What do all these accounts tell us about the nature of our spiritual warfare as Christians?

- Describe scenes where Samson's strength was highlighted in this lesson. Did Samson use his strength faithfully or unfaithfully in these scenes?

  If you are in a group, read Numbers 6:6. From your reading, what may be an implication of Samson's eating the honey out of the carcass of a lion? Why do you think Samson did not tell his parents where the honey came from when he gave it to them to eat?

- What do you consider to be the fundamental lesson from Samson's violent exploits?

If you are in a group, have each member identify one or two characters in the Bible whose sin is never glossed over by the biblical writers. What does this teach us about God?

PRAYER

- Praise God for His omnipotent ability to bring about His will despite man's sin.
- Confess any times in your life when you have lived by sight and not by faith.
- Thank God for the ways He has intervened in your life to keep you from sin.
- Ask God to continually show you by His Spirit the way out of temptation.

REVIEW QUIZ

1. In act 2, what prominent theme is introduced after Samson begins to pursue his wife?
   a. Sight
   b. Justice
   c. Violence
   d. Righteousness

2. What city does Samson go to in order to pursue his wife?
   a. Zorah
   b. Gibeah
   c. Timnah
   d. Ashkelon

3. Which of the following statements best summarizes the lesson Samson should have learned from his riddle about the lion?
   a. Strength would be all that was needed to defeat the Philistines.
   b. Consecration would be maintained by Spirit-empowered strength.
   c. Strength would be the means for peace between Israel and the Philistines.
   d. Consecration would be the process in which the bitterness of death leads to life.

4. How many changes of clothing were wagered in the Samson's riddle?
   a. 45
   b. 30
   c. 20
   d. 15

5. Samson's wife willingly presented a plan to the Philistines of persuading Samson to give her the answer to the riddle during the wedding feast.
    a. True
    b. False

6. What does Samson's reaction to losing the wager reveal about Samson?
    a. Samson was willing to use his strength for selfish and ungodly ends.
    b. Samson was beginning to recognize his call as a judge to deliver Israel.
    c. Samson was unwilling to continue along with the plan of marrying a Philistine.
    d. Samson was beginning to repent of his tendency toward self-indulgence.

Answer Key—The Selfishness of Samson

REFLECTION & DISCUSSION QUESTIONS

🕐 Before the Video

What Do You Think?

These are personal questions. The answers should be based on your own knowledge and experience.

Scripture Reading

- How has Samson thus far demonstrated the qualities of someone who loves the world?

  Samson has thus far demonstrated the qualities of someone who loves the world by following the desires of his eyes in pursuing a wife from the Philistines instead of obeying the Word of God.

🕐 During the Video

Samson's Riddle

- What was the riddle that Samson put to the Philistines?

  Samson was inspired to create a riddle from his encounter with the lion: "Out of the eater came something to eat. Out of the strong came something sweet" (Judg. 14:14).

- What lesson may God have been teaching Samson from his experience with the lion? What truth did Samson miss from his very own riddle?

  God may have been teaching Samson a lesson about his calling to be consecrated in the power of the Spirit when he encountered the lion. It was perhaps a moment for Samson to reconsider what he was doing in marrying a Philistine woman. Samson also missed an important lesson from his very own riddle that out of death comes life. Samson should have been dying to self in order to experience the fullness of life in the Lord.

The Viciousness of Sin

- What was the wager of Samson's riddle? Was it a significant wager? Why?

  Samson wagered that he would give the Philistine men thirty undergarments and thirty changes of clothing if they could answer his riddle, and these men would likewise give Samson thirty undergarments and thirty changes of clothing if they were unable to answer his riddle. This wager was significant because clothing was expensive at the time and would have been especially costly for Samson.

- How does violence escalate in act 2 of Samson's story?

  To begin with, we may consider Samson's encounter with the lion as a violent encounter, but the violence escalates significantly when the Philistine men threaten Samson's wife. When Samson loses the wager of his riddle, he kills thirty Philistines in order to fulfill his end of the bargain, heightening the violence of act 2 even further.

- How does the end of this lesson suggest that a cycle of violence and revenge will continue in the remainder of act 2 in Samson's story?

  At the end of this lesson, Samson's wife has been given to another man by her father. Because of this, Samson feels justified in his anger and declares, "This time I shall be innocent in regard to the Philistines, when I do them harm" (Judg. 15:3).

⏱ After the Video

- How was Samson able to defeat the lion on his journey to the marriage feast?

  Samson is described to have torn the lion to pieces with his bare hands "as one tears a young goat" (Judg. 14:6). This was the first significant feat of Samson's strength that we are told about, and it was only made possible because "the Spirit of the LORD rushed upon him" (Judg. 14:5).

- Describe scenes where Samson's strength was highlighted in this lesson. Did Samson use his strength faithfully or unfaithfully in these scenes?

  Two scenes of Samson's strength were narrated in this lesson: the scene with the lion and the scene with the Philistine men. In the scene with the Philistine men, it is obvious that Samson used his strength unfaithfully. He only used his strength for his own vengeful self-indulgence to pay the price of losing the wager from his riddle.

- What do you consider to be the fundamental lesson from Samson's violent exploits?

  The answers to these questions should express what you consider to be a primary lesson Samson's violence might teach us. Dr. Godfrey noted that perhaps the most important lesson we learn from such violence is that God was still working through him for good, which will be developed further in the next lecture.

REVIEW QUIZ

1. **C.**
   Act 2 begins with the theme of sight with Samson's choice of a wife who was right in his own eyes. After Samson begins to pursue his wife, the prominent theme of violence is introduced to the story, as found both in the violence of the Philistines and in the violence of Samson himself.

2. **C.**

Samson traveled to Timnah to pursue his wife, which of course was a Philistine city in Canaan. The comments of Samson's parents and his recalcitrance in pursuing a Philistine woman in Timnah function as an overt commentary on Samson's folly.

3. **D.**

Samson's riddle about the honey in the lion should have taught him a lesson about the nature of his consecration. Samson, at this point in his life, can be characterized by self-indulgence, so the nature of his consecration at this point in his life could be best described as a dying to self. Just as with the lion and the honey, only out of this death would come the sweetness of life.

4. **B.**

Thirty changes of clothing were wagered over Samson's riddle. If we also include the thirty undergarments, this was a pricey wager, especially for Samson. If he were to lose the bet, he would have to provide all of these garments himself as opposed to the thirty men providing them.

5. **B.**

Samson's wife did not present a plan to the Philistines out of her own volition. Rather, she was threatened, along with her family, by the Philistines. It was only after being coerced that she persuaded Samson to give her the answer to the riddle.

6. **A.**

When Samson lost the wager, he reacted by killing thirty Philistine men in order to fulfill the wager. This demonstrates that Samson was willing to use the strength that God gave him for his own selfish and vengeful ends, which is uncharacteristic of one who was to be set apart for the Lord.

6

The Calling of Samson

INTRODUCTION

The escalating violence in Samson's life points to the seriousness of Samson's disobedience, yet God was still raising up Samson to be a judge in Israel. The consequences of Samson's sin actually became the catalyst for his concern for Israel. In this lesson, Dr. Godfrey continues to narrate the episodes of act 2 in Samson's life to show how God is able to use people despite their sin.

LEARNING GOALS

When you have finished this lesson, you should be able to:

- Identify the providential hand of God in Samson's life
- Detail Samson's journey in becoming a judge in Israel

KEY IDEAS

- God created an opportunity against the Philistines through Samson's disobedience.
- Samson assumed the role of judge through a mighty act of deliverance on behalf of Israel.
- The end of act 2 gives us a glimpse of Samson's faith and reveals an important principle of prayer.

REFLECTION & DISCUSSION QUESTIONS

🕐 Before the Video

What Do You Think?

- If God is able to use even a person's sin for His own glory, should we still fight against sin in our own lives? Why or why not?

- Do you give God reasons why He should answer your prayers? Why or why not?

Scripture Reading

Make me know your ways, O LORD; teach me you paths. Lead me in your truth and teach me, for you are the God of my salvation; for you I wait all the day long. Remember your mercy, O LORD, and your steadfast love, for they have been from of old. Remember not the sins of my youth or my transgressions; according to your steadfast love remember me, for the sake of your goodness, O LORD!

—Psalm 25:4–7

- What sort of appeals to God does David make so that God might answer his prayer? Take a moment to pray using this passage of Scripture as a model.

⏱ During the Video

▶ *Play the video; pause at 7:58.*

The Violence Continues

- How is the episode with the foxes both comedic and tragically ironic?
- What did Samson want to do after taking revenge upon the Philistines?
- In what way was God beginning to move Samson away from his selfishness?

▶ *Play the video to the end.*

An Important Principle of Prayer

- What important principle of prayer is revealed in Samson's prayer after he defeated the Philistines?
- What was the appeal Samson made so that God might answer his prayer?
- How did God answer Samson's prayer?

⏱ After the Video

- What was the first thing the men of Judah said to Samson when they came to hand him over to the Philistines? What does this indicate?

  If you are in a group, think back on lesson 2 and discuss the significance the tribe of Judah plays in the book of Judges. How is the overall trajectory of the book of Judges reinforced by the intimidation of the three thousand men of Judah?

- How does Samson begin to lead the people of Israel? What is the significance of Samson's finding "a fresh jawbone of a donkey" (Judg. 15:15)?

  If you are in a group, discuss some of the other incidents of foreshadowing encountered thus far in Samson's story. What effect do the foreshadowing and seemingly repeated scenes in Samson's story have on you?

- In all of act 2, where is Samson's faith the most evident?

  If you are in a group, discuss the different ways one could think about Samson's prayer based on what we know about his character. Do you think Samson is a changed man?

PRAYER

- Praise God for His steadfast love and mercy as a deliverer of His people.
- Confess any time in which you have let your sin intimidate and define you.
- Thank God for the help He has provided even when you have felt helpless.
- Ask God to encourage and strengthen you in your faith for His name's sake.

REVIEW QUIZ

1. Why did Samson's attack on the Philistines with the foxes provoke such harsh retaliation?
   a. The Philistines were deeply offended because they worshiped foxes.
   b. The Philistines were humiliated by being bested by the foxes.
   c. The Philistines relied on the crops burned by the foxes.
   d. The Philistines did nothing to provoke Samson's attack by the foxes.

2. Why was Samson in hiding after taking revenge on the Philistines for his wife?
   a. Samson was recovering his strength.
   b. Samson was fleeing from the men of Judah.
   c. Samson was plotting a way to become a judge.
   d. Samson was attempting to end the cycle of retaliation.

3. When the men of Judah handed Samson over to the Philistines, what was being foreshadowed by the Philistines' reaction?
   a. Samson's encounter with Delilah
   b. Samson's reign as a judge over Israel
   c. Samson's moral failure with a Philistine prostitute
   d. Samson's victory over the Philistines in the temple of Dagon

4. Who are the men of Judah comparable to in Samson's story?
   a. Samson's wife
   b. Samson's father
   c. Samson's mother
   d. Samson's father-in-law

5. We are not told how many Philistines Samson killed when he took vengeance for the death of his Philistine wife and father-in-law.
   a. True
   b. False

6. How many years does Samson rule as a judge over Israel?
    a. 40
    b. 30
    c. 20
    d. 10

Answer Key—The Calling of Samson

🕐 Before the Video

What Do You Think?

These are personal questions. The answers should be based on your own knowledge and experience.

Scripture Reading

- What sort of appeals to God does David make so that God might answer his prayer? Take a moment to pray using this passage of Scripture as a model.

  David makes a number of different appeals to God so that God might answer his prayer in Psalm 25. David first highlights his relationship with God, both his knowledge of God as the God of his salvation and the fact that he waits for God "all the day long." David then appeals to God's very own character, that God would answer his prayer for the sake of His mercy, love, and goodness.

🕐 During the Video

The Violence Continues

- How is the episode with the foxes both comedic and tragically ironic?

  The episode with the foxes begins in a comedic fashion because of the idea of Samson gathering so many fast and nimble foxes, but then the episode turns tragically ironic when Samson's actions result in his wife and father-in-law being burned alive. The irony can be seen in her identification with the Philistines as "my people" (Judg. 14:16). In the end, it was her very own people who killed her.

- What did Samson want to do after taking revenge upon the Philistines?

  After Samson's Philistine wife and father-in-law were burned alive, Samson was again resolved to take revenge upon the Philistines. Samson's hope after taking revenge upon them was to quit the cycle of violence entirely (Judg. 15:7).

- In what way was God beginning to move Samson away from his selfishness?

  God was beginning to move Samson away from his selfishness through the magnitude of the Philistine retaliation on Samson's actions. The Philistines rallied an army and began to raid the people of Israel at Lehi. Samson's actions were of such consequence that they now involved the people of Israel, so Samson began to assume a role as a leader for Israel's benefit.

An Important Principle of Prayer

- What important principle of prayer is revealed in Samson's prayer after defeating the Philistines?

  After defeating the Philistines, Samson was thirsty nearly to the point of death if he were to be overtaken in battle, so he called out to the Lord in prayer. His prayer reveals a very important principle that should inform all our prayers: that we ought to give God reasons why He should answer our prayers.

- What was the appeal Samson made so that God might answer his prayer?

  Samson appealed to God's very own reputation as the rationale for why God should answer his prayer. Samson had been given a great victory; was he now to die at the hand of the uncircumcised? Samson understood that such a shameful death would not bring God's name glory, so he invoked God's covenantal nature, calling the Philistines "the uncircumcised" (Judg. 15:18).

- How did God answer Samson's prayer?

  God answered Samson's prayer by miraculously splitting open the hollow place at Lehi. Samson was given water to drink and his spirit was revived (Judg. 15:19).

⏱ After the Video

- What was the first thing the men of Judah said to Samson when they came to hand him over to the Philistines? What does this indicate?

  The men of Judah confronted Samson about his conquests against the Philistines by first asking him, "Do you not know that the Philistines are rulers over us?" This indicates that even the tribe of Judah felt helpless against the Philistines and that all of Israel felt resigned to defeat.

- How does Samson begin to lead the people of Israel? What is the significance of Samson's finding "a fresh jawbone of a donkey" (Judg. 15:15)?

  Samson begins to lead the people of Israel by taking an authoritative role with the men of Judah. Samson does this by asserting himself and demanding that the men of Judah make a vow to him that they will not attack him themselves (Judg. 15:12). After being handed over to the Philistines, Samson uses a jawbone to kill the Philistines. The jawbone itself does not have any significance (beside being a nice comical touch to the story), but it is significant that we are told that it is a "fresh" jawbone, unaffected by the arid climate.

- In all of act 2, where is Samson's faith the most evident?

  One could argue that Samson's faith can be clearly seen when he fights victoriously against the Philistines in the power of the Spirit, but his faith is most evident when he prays to God. It is here that we begin to see Samson's dependence on God and his understanding of the true source of his strength.

REVIEW QUIZ

1. **C.**

   The retaliation of the Philistines was harsh and ruthless because Samson's attack by means of the foxes was aimed at the Philistines' means of sustenance. The foxes burned the Philistine crops, which they needed to survive the winter.

2. **D.**

   The violence in act 2 has escalated one scene after another. Samson desired to put an end to his feud with the Philistines after first avenging his Philistine wife (Judg. 15:7), but the Philistines continued the cycle by forming an army to attack Israel.

3. **D.**

   The rejoicing of the Philistines when they saw Samson bound and delivered by the men of Judah foreshadows the rejoicing of the Philistines at the temple of Dagon. In both scenes, the Philistines will be defeated.

4. **C.**

   The men of Judah are most comparable to Samson's mother. Remember the beginning of Samson's story and the barrenness of Samson's mother. Unlike Hannah, Samson's mother does not pray for her barrenness but rather accepts her condition. The men of Judah are like her in that they have resigned themselves to the rule of the Philistines.

5. **A.**

   Samson desired revenge for the death of his Philistine wife and father-in-law. We are told that Samson took his vengeance upon the Philistines by striking them "hip and thigh with a great blow" (Judg. 15:8), but we are not told the number of men who received this blow. Samson's battle with a donkey's jawbone is an entirely different account.

6. **C.**

   Samson reigned in Israel twenty years during the period of the Philistines. His first great act as judge was perhaps the slaughter of the Philistines with the donkey's jawbone.

7

The Foolishness of Samson

INTRODUCTION

Samson reigned as a judge in Israel for twenty years, yet we are not told about the quality of his rule during this period. What we do know is that Samson would eventually fall back into his foolish ways. In this lesson, Dr. Godfrey walks us through Samson's encounter with a prostitute as the summary statement of his judgeship and introduces Samson's ultimate folly with Delilah.

LEARNING GOALS

When you have finished this lesson, you should be able to:

- Recognize the ways in which Samson represents Israel
- Identify the significant details of act 3 in Samson's story
- Detail the extent of Samson's foolishness with Delilah in act 4

KEY IDEAS

- Samson's rule as a judge is summarized by his encounter with a Philistine prostitute.
- Samson's foolishness is manifested in his continued relations with Philistine women, most particularly in his love for Delilah.

REFLECTION & DISCUSSION QUESTIONS

🕐 Before the Video

What Do You Think?

- What sort of details would you consider important to include in a narration of Samson's twenty-year reign as a judge in Israel?
- In what areas has Samson exhibited foolishness up to this point in his life? What should he have learned from his past mistakes?

Scripture Reading

O God, do not keep silence; do not hold your peace or be still, O God! For behold, your enemies make an uproar; those who hate you have raised their heads. They lay crafty plans against your people; they consult together against your people; they consult together against your treasured ones. They say, "Come, let us wipe them out as a nation; let the name of Israel be remembered no more!"

—Psalm 83:1–4

- What does Psalm 83 reveal to us about Israel's experiences in history? Against whom are the enemies of God's people ultimately fighting?

⏱ During the Video

▶ *Play the video; pause at 12:30.*

The Sum of Samson's Rule

- What hint is given in act 3 that God had given Samson success as a judge in Israel?
- How is the episode in Gaza an impressive demonstration of Samson's strength?
- What is historically significant about the city to which Samson carried the city gates?

▶ *Play the video to the end.*

Samson and Delilah

- The lords of the Philistines asked Delilah to "seduce" Samson. What translation of this word did Dr. Godfrey suggest is more accurate?
- Was Delilah deceptive or honest with Samson when she asked him about his strength? What does this suggest about Samson?
- How does the narrator of Judges build tension in Samson's interactions with Delilah?

⏱ After the Video

- In what way is Samson representative of Israel in act 3?

  If you are in a group, create a list of qualities that characterize Samson as a judge in light of Israel's hardships and spiritual failures during the period of the judges. Then, compare this list with the list you created for Deborah in lesson 2. What are some key differences between Samson (Israel) and Deborah?

- What are the similarities and differences between the story of Samson's wife requesting the answer to Samson's riddle and Delilah requesting the source of Samson's strength?

  If you are in a group, discuss the way Samson's wife and Delilah felt towards

Samson. Is there any indication in the stories about how each of them felt toward Samson? Consider the ways Samson's wife and Delilah were approached by men to be used against Samson.

- Why do you think the narrator of Judges represents the entirety of Samson's rule as a judge in a mere three verses in Judges 16:1–3?

  If you are in a group, have each member share what they hope would be said of their life in the form of a summary statement. What qualities would you want others to consider outstanding and exemplary of your life?

PRAYER

- Praise God for His mercy in providing perfect righteousness in Christ.
- Confess your failure to use biblical wisdom in every one of your decisions.
- Thank God for preserving you through difficult circumstances caused by your sin.
- Ask God to use you as an instrument to direct others away from the blindness of sin.

REVIEW QUIZ

1. As highlighted by Dr. Godfrey, what overarching theme is reintroduced in act 3?
   a. The theme of strength
   b. The theme of shame
   c. The theme of sight
   d. The theme of sin

2. According to Dr. Godfrey, in what way does Samson represent Israel in act 3?
   a. By receiving mercy from God through escape
   b. By doing what was right in his own eyes
   c. By having illicit sexual engagements
   d. By being surrounded by enemies

3. Where did Samson carry the Philistine gates as a demonstration of his great strength?
   a. Gaza
   b. Hebron
   c. Gibeah
   d. Jerusalem

4. What does Delilah's name mean?
   a. Lovely
   b. Envious
   c. Flirtatious
   d. Delightful

5. We know for certain that act 3 takes place in the first five years of Samson's judgeship.
   a. True
   b. False

6. Considering what you know about how Philistia was governed, how many pieces of silver would Delilah be given if each of the lords of Philistia offered her 1,100 pieces?
   a. 2,200
   b. 4,400
   c. 5,500
   d. 7,700

Answer Key—The Foolishness of Samson

🕐 Before the Video

What Do You Think?

These are personal questions. The answers should be based on your own knowledge and experience.

Scripture Reading

- What does Psalm 83 reveal to us about Israel's experiences in history? Against whom are the enemies of God's people ultimately fighting?

  Psalm 83 reveals that Israel's experience in history has been marked by opposition, such that even nations are named in the wider context of Psalm 83 to enumerate upon all the enemies of God's people. Ultimately, the enemies of God's people are fighting against God Himself, even making a covenant with one another against Him (Ps. 83:5).

🕐 During the Video

The Sum of Samson's Rule

- What hint is given in act 3 that God had given Samson success as a judge in Israel?

  The fact that Samson willfully went into Gaza, a city of the Philistines, gives us a hint at the success Samson had enjoyed as a judge in Israel. He was able to enter a Philistine city unafraid.

- How is the episode in Gaza an impressive demonstration of Samson's strength?

  It is impressive on multiple levels. First, the Philistines presumed that Samson would not be able to leave the city until dawn, which tells us something about the strength of the city's gates, especially in a capital city in Philistia. Second, Samson carried the gates to Hebron, which was about thirty miles away from Gaza and the highest city in Israel.

- What is historically significant about the city to which Samson carried the city gates?

  Samson carried Gaza's city gates to Hebron, the city in which David was twice anointed king, first of Judah and then of all Israel. This city was also near Abraham's place of burial, which could have been a reminder of God's covenant protection.

Samson and Delilah

- The lords of the Philistines asked Delilah to "seduce" Samson. What translation of this word did Dr. Godfrey suggest is more accurate?

  Dr. Godfrey suggested that the word "seduce" in Judges 16:5 could be better translated as "deceive." The lords of the Philistines were asking Delilah to do something broader than seduction. They wanted her to deceive Samson that she actually loved him.

- Was Delilah deceptive or honest with Samson when she asked him about his strength? What does this suggest about Samson?

  On the one hand, Delilah was deceiving Samson. On the other hand, she was quite honest in the way she asked Samson about his strength. She asked him plainly for the source of his strength and how he might be subdued, which points to Samson's foolishness and total liability in his downfall.

- How does the narrator of Judges build tension in Samson's interactions with Delilah?

  The narrator of Judges builds tension in the final act of Samson's story by detailing the ways that Samson misleads Delilah about the true source of his strength. After each of his fabrications, Delilah attempts to subdue him to no avail, adding a touch of comedic tension to the story.

⏱ After the Video

- In what way is Samson representative of Israel in act 3?

  In act 3, Samson is representative of Israel in regard to the way various peoples sought to destroy Israel. When Samson was in Gaza, he was surrounded by Philistines seeking his life. In much the same way, Israel experienced threatening plots, which was outlined in this lecture using Psalm 83. Additionally, Samson represents Israel in his spiritual failures, being led with his eyes to a prostitute instead of being led by faith to God.

- What are the similarities and differences between the story of Samson's wife requesting the answer to Samson's riddle and Delilah requesting the source of Samson's strength?

  There are many similarities between these two stories. Both Samson's wife and Delilah pleaded for the information that they sought from Samson. They were both approached by Philistine men to deceive Samson, yet they were approached in very different ways: Samson's wife was outright threatened, and Delilah was offered silver.

- Why do you think the narrator of Judges represents the entirety of Samson's rule as a judge in a mere three verses in Judges 16:1–3?

The answer to this question is subjective, but it should be noted that the three-verse summary of Samson's rule as a judge follows the overall pattern of Samson's life: Samson follows his sinful desires into serious difficulties from which the Lord faithfully delivers him. The three-verse summary of Samson's judgeship ultimately showcases God's faithfulness to Samson in spite of Samson.

REVIEW QUIZ

1. **C.**

   Though each of these may be considered a theme in Samson's story, especially themes such as strength and sin, the theme of sight was particularly highlighted by Dr. Godfrey. Just as in act 2, when Samson saw a wife who was right in his eyes, Samson once again succumbs to the temptation of his sight, setting his eyes on another Philistine woman, this time a prostitute.

2. **D.**

   Though it can be said that Samson represents Israel in all these ways, Dr. Godfrey uses Psalm 83 to argue that Samson is representative of the profound struggle of Israel against enemy nations. The Philistines' war against Samson corresponds to Israel's history of struggle among the nations.

3. **B.**

   Samson carried Gaza's city gates to Hebron, which is significant because Hebron was about thirty miles from Gaza and it was the city with the highest elevation in Israel. Gaza was also a capital city of Philistia, so we can assume that the gates were substantial, both ornate and heavy enough to serve as a fortification for the city.

4. **C.**

   Delilah's name means "flirtatious." The meaning of Delilah's name causes one to question whether this was her real name. Either way, if it is a revelation of her character, she did not have any genuine love for Samson.

5. **B.**

   The text of Judges 16:1–3 does not tell us when act 3 takes place within Samson's rule as a judge. We only know that it took place sometime within the twenty years of his judgeship. The prepositional phrase "after this" in Judges 16:4 does not provide us with a definite sense of when act 3 takes place either.

6. **C.**

   Philistia was ruled by five different lords, who ruled five different regions out of the five capital cities of Philistia. Delilah would then have been given 5,500 pieces of silver since these rulers each offered her 1,100 pieces of silver. This was an incredible amount of money, which indicates the degree to which the Philistines wanted Samson dead.

The Humiliation of Samson

INTRODUCTION

The state of our heart is one of God's primary concerns. He calls us to love Him with all of our heart, mind, soul, and strength. The ultimate tragedy of Samson's life is that he would give his heart to Delilah when he should have given it to the Lord. In this lesson, Dr. Godfrey directly connects Samson's humiliation at the hands of the Philistines to his betrayal of the Lord.

LEARNING GOALS

When you have finished this lesson, you should be able to:

- Provide a reason why Samson lost his strength
- Describe the nature of Samson's humiliation
- Interpret Samson's prayer for strength

KEY IDEAS

- Samson's hair was a sign of strength and not a magical source of strength.
- Samson's idolatrous love for Delilah resulted in the loss of God's presence.
- The Philistines humiliated Samson by gouging out his eyes, the source of his trouble.
- Samson's prayer is ultimately a pious request that God would be glorified by vindicating him before the Philistines.

REFLECTION & DISCUSSION QUESTIONS

🕐 Before the Video

What Do You Think?

- What characterizes a heart devoted to God? How does this compare to Samson?
- What are some differences between pagan religion and biblical religion?

Scripture Reading

Hear, O Israel: The Lord our God, the Lord is one. You shall love the Lord your God with all your heart and with all your soul and with all your might. And these words that I command you today shall be on your heart. You shall teach them diligently to your children, and shall talk of them when you sit in your house, and when you walk by the way, and when you lie down, and when you rise. You shall bind them as a sign on your hand, and they shall be as frontlets between your eyes. You shall write them on the doorposts of your house and on your gates.

—Deuteronomy 6:4–9

- How does this passage describe the comprehensiveness of what Jesus considered to be the greatest commandment?

🕐 During the Video

▶ *Play the video; pause at 8:58.*

Samson Loses His Strength

- What is the fundamental sin at the heart of Samson's love for Delilah?
- What was the source of Samson's strength? Was it his hair?
- How was Delilah like Judas? How was she unlike Judas?

▶ *Play the video to the end.*

Samson's Humiliation

- Why did the Philistines gouge out Samson's eyes rather than making him a slave?
- How did the Philistines further humiliate Samson after gouging out his eyes?

🕐 After the Video

- What is ironic about Samson's humiliation?

  If you are in a group, read Psalm 107:10–16. At what points does it bring Samson to your mind, as if the psalmist was thinking about Samson as he wrote? How does this psalm remind you of Israel? In what ways does it resonate with your own experience?

- What indication does the narrator give that Samson's blindness and imprisonment aren't the end of the story?

  If you are in a group, discuss some possible interpretations of Judges 16:22. How do you understand this verse when it has been argued that there aren't any magical properties in Samson's hair that endow him with strength?

- How does Samson's prayer sound impious? Was it actually impious? Why or why not?

  If you are in a group, have each of the members reflect upon their prayer life. What are some areas to focus on in prayer to avoid impiety before God? Also, consider the times when we are told about Samson praying in his story. Are there any lessons we can learn from this about how not to pray?

PRAYER

- Praise God for His righteous judgment against sin in Christ.
- Confess any hard-heartedness that keeps you from frequent prayer.
- Thank God for being gracious and answering your prayers in times of need.
- Ask God to soften your heart so that you approach Him more swiftly for help.

REVIEW QUIZ

1. What book of the Bible did Dr. Godfrey argue is a significant theological reference point for the author of the book of Judges?
   a. Exodus
   b. Leviticus
   c. Numbers
   d. Deuteronomy

2. What sin was Samson primarily guilty of with Delilah?
   a. Covetousness
   b. Adultery
   c. Idolatry
   d. Lying

3. What is the name of the Philistine god whose temple Samson destroys?
   a. Baal
   b. Asherah
   c. Marduk
   d. Dagon

4. What did Dr. Godfrey argue is the purpose of magic in pagan religion?
   a. To give humans control of the gods
   b. To develop rituals that aid spirituality
   c. To create balance and harmony on earth
   d. To understand unseen forces in the universe

5. Delilah meets her death in the temple of Dagon after betraying Samson.
   a. True
   b. False

6. What is *not* one of Dr. Godfrey's arguments for the piety of Samson's prayer?
   a. Samson appeals to God by humbly asking to be remembered.
   b. Samson appeals to God by listing his achievements as a judge.
   c. Samson desires vindication so that God's glory might be upheld.
   d. Samson desires vindication in terms of his identity as a judge in Israel.

Answer Key—The Humiliation of Samson

REFLECTION & DISCUSSION QUESTIONS

🕒 Before the Video

What Do You Think?

These are personal questions. The answers should be based on your own knowledge and experience.

Scripture Reading

- How does this passage describe the comprehensiveness of what Jesus considered to be the greatest commandment?

  This passage describes the greatest commandment in such a way that it encompasses all of life. God's commandments are to be ever before our minds as a sign on our hands, as frontlets before our eyes, written on our doorposts and on our gates. In relation to ourselves, we are to love God with all of our being—heart, soul, and might. In relation to others, we are called to teach God's commandments to our children and to have them as the substance of our conversation throughout the day.

🕒 During the Video

Samson Loses His Strength

- What is the fundamental sin at the heart of Samson's love for Delilah?

  The fundamental sin at the heart of Samson's love for Delilah is idolatry. Samson and Delilah's relationship was essentially a spiritual battle over Samson's heart. Delilah's requests for the source of his strength were truly requests to be a god in Samson's life.

- What was the source of Samson's strength? Was it his hair?

  There was nothing magical about Samson's hair. Samson's hair was a sign of his vow to be a Nazirite, consecrated and set apart for the Lord. It was a sign of his strength, but it was not the source of his strength. The source of Samson's strength was the Lord.

- How was Delilah like Judas? How was she unlike Judas?

  Delilah was like Judas in that she was a betrayer, one who took mere silver in exchange for someone's life. Unlike Judas, she did not show any worldly sorrow for her betrayal. In fact, Judges 16:19 tells us that she played an active role in tormenting Samson before disappearing from his life.

Samson's Humiliation

- Why did the Philistines gouge out Samson's eyes instead of making him a slave?

  In the ancient world, it was common for conquerors to humiliate the leader of those who were conquered. Ancient people did this by mutilating leaders, which was symbolic and practical, because a mutilated leader could not rise up and pose a threat ever again. If Samson were an ordinary soldier, he would have perhaps been used as a slave, for it would have been of greater value to prosper from an ordinary soldier in this manner.

- How did the Philistines further humiliate Samson after gouging out his eyes?

  After gouging out his eyes, the Philistines took Samson to prison and forced him to grind grain as if he were a beast of burden. The Philistines also paraded Samson around for their entertainment while mocking him and the one true God of Israel in praise of their god, Dagon.

⏱ After the Video

- What is ironic about Samson's humiliation?

  The irony of Samson's humiliation is that the very thing that led him astray time and again would be taken away from him. Samson did what was right in his own eyes, and the Philistines would ultimately gouge them out. It was not until Samson lost his sight that he began to see clearly and once again called upon the Lord.

- What indication does the narrator give that Samson's blindness and imprisonment aren't the end of the story?

  In Judges 16:22, we are told that Samson's hair began to grow again. This little note keeps us on the edge of our seats in anticipation of what will happen next. It indicates that Samson's strength might indeed return and that the story won't end with Samson blindly grinding the mill in prison.

- How does Samson's prayer sound impious? Was it actually impious? Why or why not?

  It may seem that Samson's prayer is impious because it sounds as if it is merely a prayer for personal vengeance: Samson asked the Lord to be "avenged on the Philistines for my two eyes" (Judg. 16:30). The answers to the last two questions can express your view of Samson's prayer, but this prayer is best understood in terms of Samson's faith. At the end of his life, he went to the Lord in prayer, and the vengeance he desired was for God's justice to the end that God would be glorified in avenging him as a judge in Israel.

REVIEW QUIZ

1. **D.**
   The book of Deuteronomy plays a significant role in the theology of Judges, especially with Deuteronomy's emphasis on the heart. Dr. Godfrey argues that the author of Judges has this very thing in mind when using the language of Samson's heart in Judges 16:17.

2. **C.**
   Samson was primarily guilty of idolatry with Delilah. He gave his heart to her, as if she were a god, when he should have given his heart to the one true God. Samson's idolatry resulted in God's removing His strengthening presence.

3. **D.**
   Baal and Asherah were gods in the Canaanite pantheon. Marduk was the god of the Babylonians. Dagon was the god of the Philistines whose temple was destroyed in Samson's last great feat of strength.

4. **A.**
   The concept of magic was introduced in this lecture because the Philistines assumed that Samson's hair was a magical source of strength. Magic in pagan religion seeks to give humans control of the gods, which strikes at the heart of biblical religion, which honors God as God.

5. **B.**
   Delilah is no longer a part of Samson's story after she betrays him. There is no indication from the narrator that she died in the temple of Dagon. Dr. Godfrey argued that she wasn't in the temple but had disappeared with her money.

6. **B.**
   Samson does not appeal to God by naming any of his past works as if to move God to respond to his prayer. This would be fundamentally impious. Rather, Samson's prayer has a pious quality when we take into consideration his request to be remembered and his desire for vindication both for the sake of God's glory and for the sake of his representative role as judge in Israel.

9

The Victory of Samson

INTRODUCTION

Samson's death was a victory of faith. He glorified God more in his death than in all of his life. On the other hand, Samson would be the final judge in Israel, and the remainder of the book of Judges narrates Israel's further decline into idolatry and moral depravity. In this lesson, Dr. Godfrey surveys the final moments of Samson's life and the finale of the book of Judges.

LEARNING GOALS

When you have finished this lesson, you should be able to:

- Recognize Samson's faith in the victory won by his death
- Summarize the circumstances in Israel at the end of the book of Judges
- Apply the theology of the book of Judges to the present day

KEY IDEAS

- Samson died in faith, sacrificing himself for God's people and pointing forward to Christ.
- Samson's death marks the beginning of Israel's radical spiritual and moral decline that ominously concludes the book of Judges.
- The book of Judges ends by signaling Israel's need for a king.

REFLECTION & DISCUSSION QUESTIONS

🕐 Before the Video

What Do You Think?

- What are your general feelings about death? Was Samson's death a heroic death? Why or why not?

- What are the most important components of worship? Who decides what these are?

Scripture Reading

*And the angel of the L*ORD *appeared to the woman and said to her, "Behold, you are barren and have not borne children, but you shall conceive and bear a son. . . ."*

*And the woman bore a son and called his name Samson. And the young man grew, and the L*ORD *blessed him. And the Spirit of the L*ORD *began to stir him in Mahaneh-dan, between Zorah and Eshtaol.*

—Judges 13:3, 24–25

- What does this passage remind us about concerning Samson from the earliest stages of his life, even before he was conceived in his mother's womb?

⏱ During the Video

▶ *Play the video; pause at 4:32.*

Victory in Death

- In what ways was Samson a type of Christ? In what ways was he not a type of Christ?
- How are God's love and grace revealed at the end of Samson's story?
- What should we think about when we encounter death in the Bible?

▶ *Play the video; pause at 17:32.*

Chaos in Israel

- What is significant about the familial ties of the Levite who served before Micah's idol?
- What should Micah's idolatry cause us to reflect upon concerning the church today?
- What event caused the civil war between Israel and the tribe of Benjamin?

⏱ After the Video

- Now that we have concluded Samson's story in the book of Judges, what is your favorite episode in Samson's life? Why? If you had a favorite story about Samson before you started this series, has it changed?

  If you are in a group, have each member identify their favorite episode in Samson's life and the reasons it is their favorite.

- Two tragic vows are made in the book of Judges. Jephthah makes a tragic vow that ends in his daughter's untimely death (Judg. 11:29–40), and Israel makes a tragic vow against the tribe of Benjamin. What was Israel's vow against Benjamin, and why was it tragic?

If you are in a group, read Deuteronomy 23:21–23. What does this passage teach us about making vows before God? How does it help you comprehend the concept of a tragic or rash vow?

- How is the book of Judges spiritually challenging to Christians?

If you are in a group, have each member identify ways in which this study on the life of Samson and the book of Judges has challenged them. Feel free to focus on the difficult content of Judges or on some personal matters this book has caused you to consider.

PRAYER

- Praise God that He can use even death for the life of His people.
- Confess ways in which you put your own interests before those of others.
- Thank God for uniting you by faith to Christ and also His body, the church.
- Ask God to help you love those in your church as fathers, mothers, sisters, and brothers.

REVIEW QUIZ

1. "Wherever we read in the Old Testament about people dying and being buried, we are encouraged to think of the final resurrection." Who wrote these words on his deathbed?
   a. C.S. Lewis
   b. John Calvin
   c. Martin Luther
   d. Charles Spurgeon

2. Which biblical figure was the Levite who served Micah's idol a descendant of?
   a. Joshua
   b. Aaron
   c. Moses
   d. Samson

3. Where was God to be worshiped during the period of the judges?
   a. Bethlehem
   b. Jerusalem
   c. Gibeah
   d. Shiloh

4. How many pieces was the Levite's concubine cut into after her death in Gibeah?
   a. 6
   b. 8
   c. 10
   d. 12

5. Israel broke its vow against the tribe of Benjamin in order to preserve Benjamin's line.
   a. True
   b. False

6. Which book of the Bible informs us how to ultimately interpret Samson's life?
   a. Deuteronomy
   b. Judges
   c. Psalms
   d. Hebrews

Answer Key—The Victory of Samson

🕐 Before the Video

What Do You Think?

> *These are personal questions. The answers should be based on your own knowledge and experience.*

Scripture Reading

- What does this passage remind us about concerning Samson from the earliest stages of his life, even before he was conceived in his mother's womb?

  This passage reminds us that Samson was a child of promise and that from the earliest stages of his life he was blessed by God. The language about his growth brings to mind similar verses about Samuel and Jesus (1 Sam. 2:21; 3:19; Luke 1:80; 2:52). We are also reminded about the intimate relationship between Samson and the Spirit of the Lord. In this lesson, we will learn that Samson is buried between Zorah and Eshtaol, which should cause us to reflect upon these verses about God blessing Samson.

🕐 During the Video

Victory in Death

- In what ways was Samson a type of Christ? In what ways was he not a type of Christ?

  Samson was a type of Christ in the way that he sacrificed himself for God's people in his death. In this way, Samson modeled the type of death Christ would die. Just as Samson's death brought victory and life to Israel, so Christ's death brought victory and life to all people. Samson was not a type of Christ to the extent that he was a sinner, but even in this respect, he points us to our own need for Christ.

- How are God's love and grace revealed at the end of Samson's story?

  God's love and grace are revealed at the end of Samson's story in that Samson was not left in the rubble of the temple of Dagon with the Philistines. Instead, Samson's family came and took him to his home to bury him. Samson was buried in the Promised Land with his fathers, a demonstration of God's care for Samson.

- What should we think about when we encounter death in the Bible?

  When we encounter death in the Bible, many things can flood our minds, such as the fall and the realities of death in our own lives, but our minds should not remain there. We should think of the reality of the resurrection, resting in the encouragement that is ours in Christ.

Chaos in Israel

- What is significant about the familial ties of the Levite who served before Micah's idol?

  The Levite who served before Micah's idol was the grandson of Moses, which indicates just how far Israel had fallen, that a Levite related to Moses would establish a place of unauthorized worship to God. This is significant because of Moses' role in delivering God's law to Israel. After only a few generations, even Moses' family was failing to maintain the fundamentals of God's law.

- What should Micah's idolatry cause us to reflect upon concerning the church today?

  Micah's idolatry should cause us to reflect upon the type of worship we offer to God in our churches. It should cause us to ask ourselves whether we are worshiping God in the manner that He has prescribed. Our desire to be faithful to God in the way we worship Him is one of the most glorious aspects of the Reformed tradition.

- What event caused the civil war between Israel and the tribe of Benjamin?

  The civil war between Israel and the tribe of Benjamin resulted from the rape and murder of the Levite's concubine in the city of Gibeah. The tribe of Benjamin refused to punish the people of Gibeah for this atrocity. The people of Gibeah were also from the tribe of Benjamin, which tells us that Benjamin chose familial ties over religious ties and the requirements of the law in Israel.

⏱ After the Video

- Now that we have concluded Samson's story in the book of Judges, what is your favorite episode in Samson's life? Why? If you had a favorite story about Samson before you started this series, has it changed?

  The answer to this question should express what you considered to be your favorite episode in Samson's life and the reason that it is your favorite.

- Two tragic vows are made in the book of Judges. Jephthah makes a tragic vow that ends in his daughter's untimely death (Judg. 11:29–40), and Israel makes a tragic vow against the tribe of Benjamin. What was Israel's vow against Benjamin and why was it tragic?

  Israel vowed not to give any of its daughters to the tribe of Benjamin. This was a tragic vow because after the civil war, the tribe of Benjamin was nearly wiped out and would cease to exist if it was not given the daughters of Israel. Israel kept its vow, but at the tragic expense of Benjamin's kidnapping women from Jabesh-gilead.

- How is the book of Judges spiritually challenging to Christians?

The book of Judges challenges us to think about the degree to which we are serving our King, Jesus Christ. It forces us to ask if we are doing what is right in our own eyes and thus creating our own version of Christianity or if we are relying on Scripture to know what is pleasing to Him.

REVIEW QUIZ

1. **B.**
   The last commentary John Calvin ever wrote was his commentary on the book of Joshua. Calvin dictated these words from his deathbed in commenting on the end of the book of Joshua, which focuses on the burial of Joshua, the leader in Israel, and Eleazer, the priest in Israel.

2. **C.**
   Jonathan, the Levite who served as a priest before Micah's idol, was a descendant of Moses. He was the son of Gershom, Moses and Zipporah's firstborn. The fact that he was a direct descendant of Moses indicates just how far Israel had fallen during the period of the judges.

3. **D.**
   God was to be worshiped in Shiloh during the period of the judges. This was where the tabernacle of God was erected before the temple was built in Jerusalem. It was therefore in Shiloh where the Levites offered authorized sacrifice to God.

4. **D.**
   After her violent death in Gibeah, the Levite's concubine was cut into twelve pieces, a piece for each of the twelve tribes of Israel. This was done in order to call Israel to seek justice against the men of Gibeah. The tribe of Benjamin refused to pursue any reprisal against Gibeah, resulting in civil war in Israel.

5. **B.**
   Israel did not break its vow against the tribe of Benjamin, which was to withhold the daughters of Israel from Benjamin so that the tribe would cease to exist. Instead, Israel devised a way around breaking its vow by allowing the men of Benjamin to kidnap women from Jabesh-gilead.

6. **D.**
   Throughout this series, Dr. Godfrey has mentioned many places in Scripture where Samson may be alluded to, but he is only explicitly mentioned in the book of Judges and the book of Hebrews. It is in Hebrews where we learn that Samson's life is an example of faith (Heb. 11:32). For this reason, Hebrews informs how we are to interpret Samson's life.

The Christian Context for Samson

INTRODUCTION

The New Testament teaches us how to rightly understand Samson. The book of Hebrews makes Samson an example of faith, such that we are to follow him insofar as we are following Christ. In this lesson, Dr. Godfrey provides an overview of the book of Hebrews in light of our study on Samson so that we might embrace the life lived by faith and not by sight.

LEARNING GOALS

When you have finished this lesson, you should be able to:

- Identify some of the major themes in the book of Hebrews
- Analyze the story of Samson from the perspective of the New Testament

KEY IDEAS

- The book of Hebrews was written to encourage first-century Jewish Christians to endure in the Christian faith.
- The story of Samson and the book of Hebrews give us a spiritual picture of the Christian life in which God's strength is made perfect in our weakness.
- The faithful saints of the Old Testament teach us to live sanctified before Christ, whom we know in a deeper and more intimate way than all those who came before Him.

REFLECTION & DISCUSSION QUESTIONS

🕐 Before the Video

What Do You Think?

- What is the nature of faith? How would you define it?
- When in your life has God manifested His strength through your weakness?

Scripture Reading

Therefore, since we are surrounded by so great a cloud of witnesses, let us also lay aside every weight and sin which clings so closely, and let us run with endurance the race that is set before us, looking to Jesus, the founder and perfecter of our faith, who for the joy that was set before him endured the cross, despising the shame, and is seated at the right of the throne of God.

—Hebrews 12:1–2

- Considering how this passage follows the section in which the author of Hebrews uses Samson as an example of faith, what is Samson's example intended to incite within us?

🕐 During the Video

▶ *Play the video; pause at 7:27*

The Book of Hebrews

- Why was the book of Hebrews written?
- How does the book of Hebrews characterize faith? How is this important to the concerns of the letter's first-century audience?

▶ *Play the video to the end.*

Samson in Hebrews

- How does Dr. Godfrey contrast Samson with Moses?
- At what points in his life does Samson demonstrate the principle that strength comes out of weakness?
- What did Dr. Godfrey give as the reason that the world was not worthy of Samson?
- What should Samson remind us about concerning our calling as Christians?

🕐 After the Video

- Since the book of Hebrews addresses the needs of first-century Jewish Christians who were tempted to return to Judaism, how does Hebrews present Christ in light of such temptation?

  If you are in a group, discuss how the struggles of the first-century audience of the book of Hebrews might be analogous to struggles in the church in the twenty-first century. What sorts of things attract Christians away from the simplicity of the faith?

- Read Hebrews 11:32–38. What connections are there to the acts of faith mentioned in Hebrews 11:32–38 and the events of Samson's life?

If you are in a group, have the members discuss Hebrews 11:32–38 further. What other biblical figures came to mind when reading Hebrews 11:32–38? How does this text contribute to the overall picture the book of Hebrews gives us of the Christian life?

- Reflect upon the learning goals you had when you began this series. Have your reached those goals? What was the most interesting concept you learned? Will it influence your life? How?

If you are in a group, have each member identify the most interesting new concept they learned in studying the life of Samson.

PRAYER

- Praise God for the grace of knowing Christ at this moment in redemptive history.
- Confess to God your tendencies to depend on your own strength instead of His.
- Thank God for giving us examples of true faith throughout the Bible and church history.
- Ask God to apply these examples so that you might also demonstrate a holy life of faith.

REVIEW QUIZ

1. Which of the following is *not* a reason why Jewish Christians in the first century may have been tempted to return to Judaism?
   a. Judaism was a legal religion within the Roman Empire.
   b. Judaism was visibly impressive with the glory of the temple.
   c. Christianity was favoring gentile believers over Jewish believers.
   d. Christianity was insignificant in terms of the number of its adherents.

2. Why did Dr. Godfrey say that Christianity seems to be split in two in our day?
   a. Justification and election have been separated.
   b. Justification and adoption have been separated.
   c. Justification and glorification have been separated.
   d. Justification and sanctification have been separated.

3. The Old Testament saints listed in Hebrews 11 did not receive the promise of God in their lifetimes. What was that promise?
   a. Land
   b. Jesus
   c. Peace
   d. Heaven

4. What concept did Dr. Godfrey use the Apostle Paul as an example of in this lecture?

   a.   Knowing Christ
   b.   Faith in the unseen
   c.   Strength in weakness
   d.   Fleeing from the pleasures of sin

5.   The Bible teaches that God is forgiving and merciful yet avenges wrongdoing.
   a.   True
   b.   False

6.   According to Dr. Godfrey, when do we see Christ in ways that people like David did not?
   a.   In the shadows of the Old Testament
   b.   In the second coming of Christ
   c.   In the fellowship of the saints
   d.   In the preaching of His Word

Answer Key—
The Christian Context for Samson

REFLECTION & DISCUSSION QUESTIONS

🕐 Before the Video

What Do You Think?

> *These are personal questions. The answers should be based on your own knowledge and experience.*

Scripture Reading

- Considering how this passage follows the section in which the author of Hebrews uses Samson as an example of faith, what is Samson's example intended to incite within us?

  Samson's example is intended to incite within us a desire to lay aside our sin such that we endure faithfully in the Christian life. Ultimately, Samson's example is intended to point us to Jesus Christ, who as our Mediator set a perfect example of the faith that endures unto glory.

🕐 During the Video

The Book of Hebrews

- Why was the book of Hebrews written?

  The book of Hebrews was written to encourage first-century Jewish Christians to endure in the faith, to keep them from abandoning the truth of the gospel by returning to Judaism.

- How does the book of Hebrews define faith? How is this important to the concerns of the letter's first-century audience?

  The book of Hebrews defines faith as the "assurance of things hoped for, the conviction of things not seen" (Heb. 11:1). This is important to the concerns of the letter's audience because it speaks directly to their needs and their temptation to leave the Christian faith and return to Judaism. It teaches these Christians not to look at the mere appearances of Judaism, such as the temple, but to look to the substance of these things, which is Christ.

Samson in Hebrews

- How does Dr. Godfrey contrast Samson with Moses?

  Dr. Godfrey contrasts Samson with Moses by highlighting Moses' faithfulness in uniting himself with God's people rather than enjoying the "fleeting pleasures of sin" in the courts of Pharaoh (Heb. 11:24–25). Unlike Moses, Samson often succumbed to these fleeting pleasures by living by sight and not by faith.

- At what points in his life does Samson demonstrate the principle that strength comes out of weakness?

  This principle is prominently demonstrated at two points in Samson's life. Both of these points were marked by prayer: when Samson called upon the Lord for water after he had defeated one thousand Philistines with a jawbone of a donkey and when Samson called upon the Lord before defeating even more Philistines in his death.

- What did Dr. Godfrey give as the reason that the world was not worthy of Samson?

  Dr. Godfrey argued that the world was not worthy of Samson because Samson, for all his faults, was a sinner saved by grace. The world was not worthy of Samson as a sinner saved by grace because God removes such sinners out of the pattern of this world in holy service for Him.

- What should Samson remind us about concerning our calling as Christians?
  Samson should remind us that we are called to live by faith and not by sight, that we are called to live by promise, and that we are called to live in Christ.

⏲ After the Video

- Since the book of Hebrews addresses the needs of first-century Jewish Christians who were tempted to return to Judaism, how does Hebrews present Christ in light of such temptation?

  Christ is presented in the book of Hebrews in such a way as to help Jewish Christians see that He is the fulfillment of the types and shadows of the Old Testament. Christ is therefore presented as the better temple, the better high priest, the better sacrifice, and the author of a better covenant. With Christ presented in this manner, these Christians could know that they had not lost any of the splendor of Judaism, which ultimately pointed to Christ.

- Read Hebrews 11:32–38. What connections are there to the acts of faith mentioned in Hebrews 11:32–38 and the events of Samson's life?

  There are many acts of faith listed in Hebrews 11:32–38. They are not all about Samson, but connections can still be made to events in his life. Samson "conquered kingdoms" in conquering the Philistines. Samson "enforced justice" and "obtained promises" relative to his role as a judge. Samson "stopped the mouths of lions" in a very literal sense when he defeated a lion on his way to Timnah. More of these connections can be made as they relate to Samson's exploits, his imprisonment, and his strength in weakness.

- Reflect upon the learning goals you had when undertaking this series. Have your reached those goals? What was the most interesting concept you learned? Will it influence your life? How?

The answers to these questions should reflect upon your own personal learning goals for this study, which you considered back in lesson 1, and they should highlight outstanding aspects of this series.

REVIEW QUIZ

1. **C.**

   Jewish Christians of the first century were not tempted to leave the faith on account of gentile favoritism. The splendor of Judaism was the real temptation. Judaism was a legal religion, so Jews were not subject to the same type of persecution that Christians were. Judaism also appeared to be more impressive than Christianity in terms of sheer numbers and, as was perhaps most persuasive to a Jewish Christian, in terms of the glory of the temple and priesthood.

2. **D.**

   Christianity can seem to be split into two parts because justification and sanctification have been separated. Those who stress justification and forget sanctification become indifferent to holiness, and those who stress sanctification at the expense of justification miss the true beauty of the gracious gospel.

3. **B.**

   The substance of all of God's promises is Christ. Whether the promise of land made to Abraham or the promise of an everlasting dynasty made to David, God fulfilled each of them in Christ. As Christians, to know Christ in a way that Abraham and David could only anticipate is one of our greatest privileges.

4. **C.**

   Dr. Godfrey used the Apostle Paul as a principal example of strength in weakness. This concept is extensively developed by Paul in 2 Corinthians, where he warns the Corinthians about the "super apostles" by highlighting the way God works through weakness. It is in this letter that we find the perennial text on finding strength in weakness: "My grace is sufficient for you, for my power is made perfect in weakness" (2 Cor. 12:9).

5. **A.**

   God is righteous to judge and avenge wrongdoing. God is also forgiving and merciful. These truths about God's character were the foundation of Dr. Godfrey's emphasis that we are to pursue holiness and never become indifferent to sin.

6. **D.**

   Dr. Godfrey stressed that, as Christians, we have actually seen Christ in the preaching of His Word, in the preaching of the gospel. Old Testament saints, such as David, did not know Christ in the fullest revelation of His person. In this we can be assured that Christ is not a distant Savior, and He is displayed before us every time the gospel is preached.